The Michigan Reader

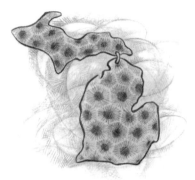

for Boys and Girls

By Kathy-jo Wargin
Illustrated by K.L. Darnell

Sleeping Bear Press

Sleeping Bear Press
310 North Main Street
P.O. Box 20
Chelsea, MI 48118
www.sleepingbearpress.com

Printed and bound in Canada.

10 9 8 7 6 5 4 3 2 1

Library of Congress Cataloging-in-Publication Data

Wargin, Kathy-jo
The Michigan reader for boys and girls / written by Kathy-jo Wargin
and illustrated by Kathryn Darnell.
p. cm.
Summary: A collection of stories, poems, facts,
riddles, and more all about Michigan.
ISBN 1-58536-042-2
Michigan—Literary collections. [1. Michigan—Literary collections.]
I. Darnell, Kathryn, ill. II. Title.
PS3623.A74 M53 2001
810.8'032774'083—dc21
2001034147

Preface

Welcome to the *Michigan Reader for Boys and Girls*. I hope you will enjoy this collection of short stories, poems, and games about Michigan. Historically, primers or readers were created as books to teach reading skills to young children, as well as a way to impart simple lessons about life. In my reader, I have chosen to write simple stories, divided into parts for beginning readers, as well as more difficult stories for the advanced young reader. I also decided to include lively poems which utilize patterns, repetition, and rhyme as a way for young children to make predictions while they are reading.

As you read along, you will find many stories and poems that are easy to use as short plays or acts. For the classroom or backyard, some of the poems like "Freedom Train" or "Beaver Hats" can be performed orally by dividing the classroom or large group into small groups, each group reading either line 1, 2, or 3 of each stanza. Some poems can even be used in combination with the short story. You can even use all of them together, and have yourself an old-fashioned show.

In addition, some of the riddles, games, and stories include questions at the end, as a way for children to expand what they have just read into their own interpretation. I hope this book is a building block for many heart-to-heart conversations about our beautiful Michigan.

Most of all, I hope this book helps create many wonderful moments between a new reader and a book, a parent and a child.

Thank you to all of the educators, librarians, and teachers who assisted me during my research, and a special thank you to Mrs. Beth White, who teaches kindergarten in Petoskey, Michigan, for allowing me to use materials from her outstanding Michigan collection. Enjoy!

Your friend always,
Kathy-jo Wargin

This book is dedicated to all the Michigan boys and girls
I have met, and all the ones I dearly hope to meet.
It is also for my very special Michigan boy, Jake Wargin.

These stories are for you, my Michigan friends.

KATHY-JO WARGIN

To all the teachers and librarians who graciously lead and share.

K.L. DARNELL

Table of Contents

A Michigan Pledge
by Kathy-jo Wargin

I pledge my heart to Michigan
Two lands and four great waters
I pledge my heart to Michigan
And all her sons and daughters.

Forever I will carry
Wherever I may roam
The beauty and the friendship
Of Michigan, my true home.

cherry / apple / grape / peach

Michigan Fruit Riddles

Sometimes I am sweet,
Sometimes I am not,
That's just part of my game.
I am smaller than a plum,
I am shiny and red,
The ~~cherie~~ is my name!

Charie

I'm fuzzy and soft,
My middle is hard,
You pick me if you can reach.
I hang on a tree,
I am yellow and orange,
You guessed it, I am a *peach*.

I am hard when I'm raw,
I am soft when I'm baked,
I am crunchy and easy to eat.
I am red, I am green,
I am yellow or gold,
I am an apple, Oh what a treat!

I am small and green,
I am small and purple.
A circle is sometimes my shape.
I grow on vines,
I am juicy and neat,
You can call me a grape.

Which two fruits are small?

charie\ grape

Which two fruits are large?

peach\ apple

Which Michigan fruits are soft?

peach\apple

Which one is fuzzy?

peach

Which one is hard and crunchy?

apple

Tell me now, which one is **your** favorite?

charie

The Lighthouse Keeper

Far upon
The darkest shore
The lighthouse keeper
Shuts the door
And walks the stairs
With lantern bright
And lights the wick
To wait all night
For ships to pass
Through rocky shoals
He stirs the stove
With red-hot coals

Peering out
 With watchful eye
 At skiffs and schooners
Passing by
 Each sailors fate
 Is up to him
 The yellow light
 Shall never dim
   Upon his watch
   There is no doubt
   This beam of hope
 Will not go out
   For he does know
   Of water's foam
   And children sweet
   Who wait
   At home.

This is My Alphabet

Uppercase

A   B   C   D   E   F   G

H   I   J   K   L   M   N

O   P   Q   R   S   T   U

V   W   X   Y   Z

Lowercase

a	b	c	d	e	f	g
h	i	j	k	l	m	n
o	p	q	r	s	t	u
v	w	x	y	z		

Michigan Character Counts

I am a citizen of Michigan. I have the chance to live a life that goes beyond good. I have the chance to be filled with greatness and the winning spirit of all that is here to be shared and appreciated.

I will be **honest**. Being honest means telling the truth even when it is difficult, and encouraging others to do the same.

I will have **compassion**. I will have compassion for all living creatures. This means I will care about my family, friends, new people I have not yet met, and all other living things. They are part of my world, and I enjoy the world around me.

I will have **respect**. I shall respect myself and others. I will take care of myself, my spirit, my brain, and my body by not doing things that will hurt me. I will be thoughtful of others, as well as the property that belongs to them or me.

I will be **responsible**. I will accept responsibility with an open heart and great pride. If others trust me to be responsible, then I will behave in a responsible manner. I will take action when I must, for I have the power to make a difference in my life, in Michigan, and the world.

I will show **courage**. I will show courage
when I am not feeling brave, and do the
right thing even when I am scared about
what other people may think or say or do.
True leaders are built on courage, and
doing what is right even when they are not
feeling brave or popular.

A Little Nonsense

Gumper Doodle
Pumpkin Noodle
Chubber Wompy
Dimple Toodle

Wagger Rumpy
Pawsy Stumpy
Jumpy Bowser
Tatter Frumpy

Oh my! Who went by?

Leapy Froggen
Bumper Noggen
Wippy Dooty
Folly Woggen

Zippy Hummer
Hippo Flummer
Tippy Sneeker
Butter Thummer!

Oh no, time to go.
One more time
But not too slow!

vocabulary: Manistee / salmon
gorges / factories / beneath

The Moon and Stars in Michigan

*Let us play a game. I am the moon and you are
the stars. Night is falling upon Michigan, and
we are high above the world. What do we see?*

Moon: I see the slow and gentle
Manistee River rolling through
the night. As I shower my
light upon her wide and
glistening path, I watch
the salmon dance in
and out of the water.

Stars: We see the Black River twist and turn through gorges and falls. It rushes and rumbles without stopping, carving its way through the deep and dark forest.

Moon: I sce bright beams of light spreading out upon the Great Lakes from lighthouses that guard the shores. They stand like candles in the night, helping boats return safely to home.

Stars: We see the strong
elk bedded down for sleep,
their dark shaggy manes
blowing gently in the night breeze.

Moon: I see lights in the square
paned windows of the factories,
row upon row of windows lighting
the sidewalk beneath them. People
are coming and going through the
night, building cars while all the
land of Michigan is asleep.

Stars: Now we see one sweet child tucked beneath blankets, dreaming of boats and lakes and books and cars.

Good-night dear moon.
Good-night dear stars.
Good-night dear child.
Good-night dear Michigan.

Michigan Days

On **Monday**
    I shall put my toes
        into the warm soft sand,

On **Tuesday**
I shall climb a dune
towering so grand.

On **Wednesday**
    I shall float downstream
        in a red canoe,

On **Thursday**
  I shall look around—
    there's so much more to do!

  On **Friday** I shall pick red cherries
and sort them in my lap.

On **Saturday** I'll find a porch
and take a long sweet nap.

On **Sunday** I shall sit and think
about my summer fun,
and settle down for just one day—
for now my work is done.

Monday

Tuesday

Wednesday

Thursday

Friday

Saturday

Sunday

Michigan Months

January brings us snow,
    and frost-white window sills.
February calls us out
    to ski on winter hills.

        March is full of maple syrup
        made from maple trees,
    and April finds the trilliums
      nodding in the breeze.

May will give us tulips—
   a bouquet in every hand.
June will send the sunshine down
   to warm the farmer's land.

July is filled with people strolling
   up and down the beaches,
August finds the orchards filled
   with sweet and juicy peaches.

September comes and so does school,
October leaves are crisp and cool.

November brings the boats to shore—
get ready for their stop.
December ends, let's start once more,
and take it from the top.

Which season is the coldest?

Winter

Which season is the warmest?

Summer

Which season makes the leaves turn colors?

Fall

Which season brings us new flowers and animals?

May

Which month is your birthday?

October

Which month is your favorite?

December

vocabulary: territory / confusion / boundary
governor / volunteers / compromise / feisty

A Michigan Wolverine

Before Michigan was a state, it was called the Michigan Territory. There was confusion about the boundary lines for this territory, and one piece of land became known as the Toledo Strip. The people who lived in the area of the Toledo Strip thought the land belonged to Michigan, while the people of Ohio thought the land belonged to them.

In 1835, a very young man named Stevens T. Mason was the acting governor of the Michigan Territory. He believed that the Toledo Strip truly belonged to Michigan. He told volunteers and troops to go to the Toledo Strip and enforce the law that said the land belonged to Michigan.

Both Ohio and Michigan thought they owned the land, so they had to make a compromise. It took two years of talking about it, but finally it was agreed that Michigan would gain a new piece of land, now known as the Upper Peninsula, in exchange for giving Ohio the right to the Toledo Strip. This seemed like a fair way to solve the problem.

However, during those two years when the people of Ohio and Michigan were trying to solve this problem, some people from Ohio started to call people from Michigan "wolverines," comparing Michigan people to this hard-fighting animal.

The Fighting Wolverines

Tough and feisty
Strong and lean
I'm a fighting wolverine.

Call me Skunk-Bear
Call me mean
I'm a fighting wolverine.

Have you ever
ever seen
A Michigan
Fighting Wolverine?

Sojourner Truth

In 1864, Sojourner Truth left her home in Battle Creek, Michigan to stay in Washington, D.C. for a short while. In Washington, she found that not all people were allowed to ride in the same street-cars together. Sojourner Truth wanted people to know that a new law had been passed. This new law allowed people of all races to ride on the same streetcars. But not all people knew about this law or wanted to obey it. Some streetcar drivers would pass by Sojourner Truth as she stood in the street waiting for a ride. They did this because she was black. This was not a loving or respectful way for people to behave, so Sojourner decided she would make all people obey this new law.

Sojourner decided that each time she wanted to ride on a streetcar, she would stand and shout until the driver noticed her. Sometimes she would ring a bell or chase after the driver until he let her on. Other times she would put her hand up to the driver and shout "I want to ride, I want to ride!" Sometimes drivers would try to push Sojourner off as she was getting into the car. Other times they would tell her to sit near the horses pulling the cars.

Sojourner did not like this. She told the drivers that they were not being fair or kind, and she insisted they let her ride with everybody else. Sojourner kept telling the government what was happening, and she kept trying to ride on the streetcars even though the drivers were cruel and unkind to her. Eventually, because Sojourner kept doing the right thing, drivers were made aware of this new law, and the consequences they would face if they did not obey it. Soon, people everywhere of all races were allowed to ride the streetcars.

Sojourner Truth eventually returned to Battle Creek and continued to show people what equality meant.

Sojourner's Song

I want to ride!
I want to ride!
Standing in the road
Sojourner cried

I want to ride!
I want to ride!
Carrying her load
Sojourner tried

To climb aboard
To climb aboard
But Sojourner Truth
Was still ignored

So
She stopped them cold
She stopped them cold
Stepped into the streetcar
Brave and bold

They tossed her out
They tossed her out
But Sojourner Truth
Began to shout

I want to ride!
I want to ride!
It's my right
To have a ride

The drivers saw
They really saw
Sojourner knew
The truth of law

She was our guide
She was our guide
For the people's right
to an equal ride.

Thank you, Ms. Truth.

Grandmother's Cottage

PART ONE
Susan and David

Knock! Knock! Knock!

The children knocked at the door. Their balled-up fists began to pound harder and harder upon the old painted red door.

"Sssh, I think she's coming," said Susan.

"No, she's not," said David, "she would have answered by now."

The children sat down on the steps of their grandmother's cottage. They had walked a long way down a dirt road to get there, and now Grandmother wasn't anywhere to be found. They stared at the windows all trimmed in red and white when all of a sudden the curtain moved just a little bit. Susan looked toward the door, perhaps Grandmother was coming!

"I thought for a minute I saw the curtain move," said Susan.

"Me too," answered David.

As David spoke, the curtain moved again and the children jumped with fright.

Nobody's Home

They peered into the window but the cottage was dark and still. The curtain moved again. Susan edged away from the house. Just then, a loud boom came from inside the cottage. It sounded as if dishes were breaking on the wood floors.

The door was locked. The cottage was dark. Where was Grandmother?

Susan and David Search

David and Susan began to look around. There was noise coming from the cottage. They felt very scared. They looked toward the beach. The old silver canoe was on shore, tipped on its side the way it always is, and the old rowboat was tied to the dock.

There was an old wicker basket on the picnic table. Susan and David kneeled on chairs and peered into the basket. They were digging through the sandwiches and cookies that were inside the basket when all of a sudden they felt a hand on their back. The children froze with fright.

The Intruder

It was Grandma. "Grandma!" they cried, "where have you been?"

"I have been out picking berries for our dessert."

"But then *who* is in your cottage?"

Grandmother looked very worried. She listened by the door for just a moment, and then slowly put the key in the door. Susan could hear her own teeth chatter and David grabbed a big stick. Grandmother turned the key very slowly. She opened the door just a little bit and SCRAAAAAAM! Out raced a big, fat, hairy raccoon.

Susan, David, and Grandmother all fell to the ground and laughed while the raccoon ran away.

The Ghost

Hush, there is a ghost that lives
in a Michigan forest.
Be quiet and careful.
It is here in the forest of Presque Isle.
Hush.
It jumps from trail to trail.
It leaps over logs.
It sails through the dense woods
as quiet as a whisper.
Hush.
And in this forest
the ghost lies down to sleep.
It sleeps on the ground like a cloud
that has fallen from the sky.

Hush now children,
do not say its name out loud.
If you see it, do not catch it.
If you do, you will have bad luck forever.
That is the promise of the Michigan Ghost.

If you see it, hold it in your heart
and you will have good luck forever.
That too, is the promise
of this Michigan Ghost.
Hush. Hush. Hush.

*A deer that is all white is called an albino deer.
They are rare, but some do exist in the forests of the
Upper Peninsula. White deer usually do not live
long because they have no natural colors to hide
them in the leaves, fields, or trees of the forest.
This makes them easy prey for predators.*

vocabulary: adventure / steamship / Buffalo Harbor
Detroit / departed / carpets / banisters

A New Adventure

May 15 1872

Dear Diary,
Today we are leaving. Mother says I must
pack my trunk, for we are leaving New
York for the summer. I am quite thrilled

about our new adventure. We will leave
the Buffalo Harbor aboard a very large
steamship. I have heard father call it a
floating palace. Mother says there will be
music and dancing and grand food during
our trip to Detroit, Michigan. She says
I should bring along my finest dresses
because there is much to see and do in the
city. I wonder if the trip will seem long?
I wonder if I shall yearn for land?
Mother says many of our friends and
neighbors have since departed for the
summer, carrying their goods and trunks
with them upon the steamships that wait in
the harbor. Our ship will be a sidewheeler.
I can't wait to see it and all of the lovely
carpets and banisters it may have.

Signed,
Clara Ruth

Where is Clara Ruth going?

Amarica

What do you think it would be like to stay on a steamship?

not as good as home

What will happen when Clara Ruth gets to Detroit?

there will be lots of things to see and do.

Trunks in Tow

Full skirts swishing
Tied with a bow
Ladies are dancing
With trunks in tow!

Jackets buttoned
Faces glow
Men with caps
And trunks in tow!

Trunks in tow!
Trunks in tow!
Marching off the steamship with
Trunks in tow!

Ladies from the east coast
Standing in a row
Babies in their arms and
Trunks in tow!

Gentlemen from Illinois
Hear the whistle blow
Watch them come to Michigan
With trunks in tow!

Trunks in tow!
Trunks in tow!
Marching off the steamship with
Trunks in tow!

The White Swan
A Poem

Soft upon the silver-tide
Dip and glide, dip and glide

The silent pearl begins to ride
Side to side, side to side

Fit with feathers for a bride
White and wide, white and wide

The silent pearl upon the tide
Dip and glide, dip and glide.

vocabulary: slavery / property / journey
freedom / understood / organize
Civil War / Underground Railroad

The Underground Railroad in Michigan

PART ONE
Slavery

A long time ago, there were people who treated other people badly because of the color of their skin. These people thought that human beings with different colored skin could be bought and sold as property. When these people were bought, they were forced to do hard work for the people who bought them. They called these people slaves and the people who bought them were called slave owners. Slavery was not a nice idea, and it hurt many kind and loving families.

The Escape

Many of these slaves lived in the south-
ern part of our country, and had to escape
to the north in order to be free. Sometimes
slave owners would let slaves go free.
Other times slaves would have to sneak
away in the night when nobody was
watching. When they did, they caught a
ride on the Underground Railroad, and
this railroad went through Michigan.

A Special Railroad

The Underground Railroad was not really a railroad. There were no tracks or cars or railroad stations. The Underground Railroad was people helping people. Some people would help the escaping slaves hide from owners who might come looking for them. Others would help transport them to safe places farther north. The Underground Railroad was churches and homes that were opened up so people could have a warm place to sleep or a good meal while they were making the journey to a new life.

Michigan Heroes

One hero from Michigan helped organize many stops on the underground railroad. Her name was Sojourner Truth. Ms. Truth helped many people escape to freedom. She was born a slave, so she understood the pain and suffering that all slaves felt. There were many other heroes from Michigan, too, and they helped many people escape to places where they could be free. The Underground Railroad kept running until President Abraham Lincoln, at the end of the Civil War, freed all the slaves in our country. He and Sojourner Truth were friends.

Freedom Train

You don't need a ticket
Oh no
You don't need a ticket
To ride this train.

    You don't need money
    Oh no
    You don't need a lot of money
    To ride this train.

This train is running
Oh yea,
This train won't stop until it's there.

This train is running
Oh yea,
This train is running everywhere.

This train is people
Oh yea
This train is people holding on.

This train is moving
Oh yea
This train is moving through the dawn.

This train is love
Oh yea
This train is love for humankind.

This train is love
Oh yea
It's the best train you will find.

The Trillium
A Poem

Wake-Robin
Wake-Robin
White with petals three.

Wake-Robin
Wake-Robin
Waving back at me.

Resting in the forest
Lily-fair and sweet
What a lucky day for me
That you and I should meet.

The trillium is a large flower with three white or pink-white petals. It grows in the forests of Michigan, and is sometimes called the wake-robin.

Why do they call it the wake-robin?

_____

Why do they call it the **tri**llium?

_____

What do you want to call this pretty flower?

_____

vocabulary: autumn / voyageurs / sashes
canoes / Mackinac / uttering / comfortable
peaceful / steersman / bundles / lurched / flannel

The Fur Trader

PART ONE

Little Jacques

Little Jacques lived near a trading post in the woods of the Michigan Territory. The trading post was a small log house with a big stone fireplace. Little Jacques watched the fur traders come and go every year. Each autumn, they came with canoes filled with bundles of beads, kettles, axes, boots, and cloth to trade.

The fur traders and voyageurs brought these things to trade for beaver furs with Native Americans who lived deep in the woods of the Michigan Territory. Jacques watched the men carry heavy loads upon their shoulders. Sometimes, Jacques would help them carry these goods to the post. The voyageurs looked so grand with their sashes and caps that Jacques would try to walk like them, and talk like them. This was the one thing Jacques wanted more than anything—to be a voyageur.

Packing Up

One warm spring day, after a long hard winter of trading, the voyageurs were packing their canoes to leave for the season. Two groups of men were arguing about which group was the fastest on the water. The two groups of voyageurs sparred back and forth quite seriously, and carried on about which canoe would make it to Mackinac Island first. Jacques watched uneasily as the argument went unsettled. That night, the voyageurs ate their dinner without uttering a sound to one another.

Little Jacques Stows Away

Jacques knew the voyageurs were leaving very early in the morning, so that night, while everyone was sleeping, he crept over to the edge of the river where the canoes were packed and waiting. He looked at the two canoes, and then chose the one with the bear and the arrows etched on the sides.

Jacques could hardly wait as he made a comfortable place in the canoe. He huddled down and slid in between two bundles of beaver pelts. He took one single pelt and laid it over himself to make it look as if he were a third bundle of furs.

Early Morning

Jacques waited there all night. He was so nervous he could barely breathe. Before he knew it, he heard the footsteps of the men as they neared the canoes. One by one they each grabbed a place on a side of the canoe and began to walk it into the river. It was quite a rumble when all eight men jumped inside, knocking its birch-bark sides with great thuds and scrapes.

PART FIVE

The Journey

Ho! Ho! All of a sudden, they were off.
Jacques heard their deep voices singing
songs as they paddled the river toward
Lake Huron. Sometimes they were sad
songs and sometimes they were so happy
and joyful that Jacques wanted to sing
along. In between the songs Jacques felt
the canoe come to a rest. He smelled the
bitter smoke that came from their pipes.
He heard drops of water fall from their
paddles as they rested along the edge of
the canoe. It sounded like rainfall on a
small stream. Jacques was very comfortable beneath the soft pelts. He was so
content that finally, he fell asleep to the
rhythm of their strokes.

PART SIX

Jacques is Caught

Jacques was having a peaceful dream when all of a sudden he was jolted from his sleep. "AAAH!" he heard the steersman say. "We will never win this race, we will never win this race to Mackinac Island!" Jacques listened. The men were complaining about how slow they felt and how far ahead the other group was. They were talking about how the group that makes it to the island first will get the best food and warmest beds. "AAAH! Our canoe feels too heavy and slow!"

Jacques wanted to tell the voyageurs not to worry, that he was there to help. He wanted to tell them that he would be the best voyageur of all! Jacques burst out from beneath the beaver pelts and shouted, "I am here, I am here!"

But the surprise on the face of the voyageurs was not the sort of surprise that Little Jacques was hoping to see.

PART SEVEN

A Boy on the Boat

"What is this? A boy?" steamed one of the men. "We have a boy on our boat? We will never win now."

Other men began to shout, too. They sounded very angry at Jacques for stowing away on their boat.

Little Jacques wanted to cry but he stood firm, insisting that he could be the best voyageur of all. The steersman handed Jacques a paddle and told him to watch the others and paddle as they did.

PART EIGHT

Jacques Paddles

Jacques watched their cedar paddles dip into the water. He watched as their arms dipped in and pulled back, and dipped some more. Soon he was sitting upon the beaver bundles that once hid him, helping the voyageurs race to Mackinac Island.

1-2-3-ho! 1-2-3-ho! The canoe lurched forward. 1-2-3-ho! 1-2-3-ho! Little Jacques felt the strength of his own arms pulling and dipping, pulling and dipping. The men began to smile and sing a fast song about dancing and girls.

The canoe raced forward with ease. Soon they began to see the other canoe just a few lengths in front of them. The

steersman shouted for joy and threw his red flannel cap at Jacques. "Put it on, little voyageur," he said, "put it on."

Jacques was so proud to be one of the voyageurs that he put the cap on without missing a stroke. When he looked up he was eye to eye with the other team. Jacques put his paddle in the water as hard as he could and shouted "Ho! Ho!"

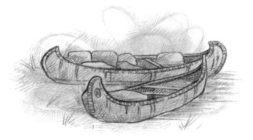

PART NINE

Mackinac Island

In moments, the canoe raced ahead of the other team and all of the men shouted for joy. They paddled and paddled with young Jacques sitting high upon the pelts, paddling too. Soon, they reached the island and pulled the canoe toward shore.

They all began to shout and dance as the water slapped at their ankles. They won! They had reached the shore before the other group of voyageurs. Tonight they would have the best food and the warmest beds. With that, the steersman pulled off his sash and tied it around Little Jacques' waist. "There, my boy, you are indeed a voyageur now. Yes, you are indeed a voyageur now."

Can You Tell Me?

Why did Little Jacques hide in the boat?

_____

How do you think Little Jacques felt when
he was hiding beneath the beaver pelts?

_____

How did the voyageurs feel when they
first noticed Jacques?

_____

What do you think Little Jacques's parents
might be thinking?

_____

Native Camps

Native camps along the shore
Hear their fires snap and roar
See the eagles as they soar
Above the water blue.

Native camps with golden light
Fires in the dark of night
Burning strong and burning bright
Beside the water true.

Where do native camps remain?
In the forest?
On the plain?

Where can native camps be found?
In the sky?
Upon the ground?

Native people standing tall
Three bold fires for them all
Hear their echoes, hold their call
Beyond the water blue.

Native camps along the shore
No more fires snap and roar
One last eagle dares to soar
Above the water blue.

vocabulary: modern / France / broad / brim
natives / bundles / backward / glance

Beaver Hats

Long ago in modern France,
    people dressed in skirts and pants,
until they thought to add instead
    a beaver hat upon their head.

The Beaver Hat
The Beaver Hat
One Broad Brim
And that is that!

So they sent the traders here
    bringing beads and battle-gear
to set up posts within the woods
    and offer natives other goods.

The Beaver Hat
The Beaver Hat
One Broad Brim
And that is that!

The natives came with beaver pelts,
    and traded them for boots and belts.
The traders piled the furs so high,
    stacks of bundles reached the sky!

The Beaver Hat
The Beaver Hat
One Broad brim
And that is that!

Then in spring they packed them all
    in canoes both big and small.
To the lake! They took their trip,
    and brought the furs to one big ship.

It sailed across the ocean wide,
    with beaver furs all tucked inside,
and then without a backward glance
    Beaver Hats all over France!

The Beaver Hat
The Beaver Hat
One Broad Brim
And that is that!

Now trading posts, they soon became
    little towns with their own name.
People opened up the woods
    by trading beaver pelts for goods.

The Beaver Hat
The Beaver Hat
One Broad Brim
And that is that!

The Key to the Kingdom of Michigan

This is the key to Michigan.
In Michigan there is a city called Detroit.
In Detroit there is a street called Green Street.
On Green Street there is a square house.
In that square house there is a yellow bed.
On that yellow bed there is a red box.
In that red box there is a tiny pouch.
In that tiny pouch there is a golden key.

Key in the pouch
Pouch in the box
Box on the bed
Bed in the house
House on the street

Street in the city
City in Michigan
And this is the key to the
Kingdom of Michigan.
Hooray!

Kathy-jo Wargin

Kathy-jo Wargin has always been drawn to the stories and poems of long ago. With a new idea in mind, she began to research many old books and primers for the types of stories that children love best. She then went on to create *The Michigan Reader for Boys and Girls*, giving a timeless idea a new twist. She is the author of many bestselling children's books, including *The Legend of the Loon*, which recently earned a Children's Choice Award from the Children's Book Council, and the newly released *The Legend of the Lady's Slipper*. Both titles are part of the Legends series from Sleeping Bear Press, which also includes *The Legend of Sleeping Bear* and *The Legend of Mackinac Island*. Other titles by Kathy-jo include *M is for Mitten: A Michigan Alphabet*, *The Michigan Counting Book*, and *L is for Lincoln: An Illinois Alphabet*.

Ms. Wargin travels frequently to speak to school children around the country, sharing ideas about the creative process, helping them find their creative spirit, and what it's like to be an author. Ms. Wargin lives in the woods of northern Michigan with her husband Ed, their son Jake, and dog Salmon.

K.L. Darnell

Artist Kate Darnell has been drawing for as long as she can remember. She earned her BFA studying drawing and painting at the University of Michigan School of Art and Design. Sleeping Bear Press published both of her previous children's books, *Fibblestax*, by Devin Scillian and *Hannah and the Homunculus*, by Kurt Hassler In addition to her work as an illustrator, Kate specializes in the beautiful art of calligraphy and is an instructor of art at Lansing Community College. She lives in East Lansing with her husband and daughter.